Taking Turns

By Janine Amos and Annabel Spenceley
Consultant Rachael Underwood

CHERRYTREE BOOKS

A Cherrytree book

Designed and produced by
A S Publishing

First published 1997
by Cherrytree Press, a division of Evans Publishing Group
2A Portman Mansions
Chiltern St
London W1U 6NR

First softcover edition 1999

Reprinted 2000, 2001, 2002, 2003, 2004

Copyright © Evans Brothers Limited 1997

British Library Cataloguing in Publication Data
Amos, Janine
   Taking Turns. - (Growing Up)
   1. Social Participation - Juvenile literature
   2. Social Interaction - Juvenile literature
   1. Title
   302.1'4

   ISBN 1 84234 009 3

Printed in Malaysia

Ben and Tim

Ben's on the bike.

Tim wants it.

Tim pushes Ben off and rides
the bike.

How do you think Tim feels?
How do you think Ben feels?

Ben cries.
He feels sad and angry.

What do you think will happen next?

Ben grabs the bike back.

Ben and Tim shout.

Gill the playworker comes over.
"Ben, you look upset," says Gill.

"And, Tim, you seem angry."

"I want the bike!" says Tim.

"I was on the bike. You pushed me.
Don't do that!" says Ben.

Ben and Tim both want the bike.
What could they do?

"Tim can have the bike when I've finished my go," says Ben.

"I'll ride round three times,"
says Ben. "Then it's your go."

"OK," agrees Tim. "I'll count."

They have worked it out.
Ben's having a turn on the bike.

Now it is Tim's turn.

They have both had a turn.
How is Ben feeling now?
How is Tim feeling?

Kate and Jo

Kate is on the slide.
She is going down on her tummy.

Jo wants to slide, too.
"Hurry up!" calls Jo.
**What do you think will happen
next?**

Jo sets off.
Kate is still on the slide.

They crash!

"That hurt me!" says Kate.
"It hurt me!" says Jo.

What could they do next time to solve the problem?

Next time Kate waves when she
has finished her turn.

And Jo waits until Kate is off the slide.

Sometimes two people want the
same thing.
That could be a problem. But
together they can work it out.

When you want a turn, tell the
other person.
Ask them to let you know when
they will be finished.
Then wait. It will be your turn soon.